SHAMBHALA POCKET LIBRARY

SONG OF MYSELF

Walt Whitman

EDITED BY
Stephen Mitchell

SHAMBHALA · Boulder · 2018

SHAMBHALA PUBLICATIONS, INC.
4720 Walnut Street
Boulder, Colorado 80301
www.shambhala.com

9 8 7 6 5 4 3 2 1

Printed in the United States of America

♾ This edition is printed on acid-free paper that meets the
American National Standards Institute z39.48 Standard.
♻ This book is printed on 30% postconsumer recycled paper.
For more information please visit us at www.shambhala.com.

Shambhala Publications is distributed worldwide by Penguin
Random House, Inc., and its subsidiaries.

THE LIBRARY OF CONGRESS CATALOGUES THE PREVIOUS EDITION
OF THIS BOOK AS FOLLOWS:
Whitman, Walt, 1819–1892. Song of myself / Walt Whitman;
edited by Stephen Mitchell.—1st Shambhala ed.
p. cm.—(Shambhala pocket classics) Includes bibliographical references (p.).
ISBN 978-0-87773-950-0 (Shambhala Pocket Classics)
ISBN 978-1-57062-369-1 (Shambhala Centaur Editions)
ISBN 978-1-61180-645-8 (Shambhala Pocket Library)
1. Whitman, Walt, 1819–1892. Song of myself— Criticism, Textual. I.
Mitchell, Stephen, 1943–
II. Title. III. Series. ps3222.s6 1993 93-20168 811.3–dc20   cip

CONTENTS

EDITOR'S PREFACE

"Song of Myself" is by far the greatest poem ever written by an American. At each rereading I feel exhilarated, as if for the first time, by its freshness and breadth of vision, its bodiliness, its high spirits, its astonishing empathy, by the freedom and goofiness and dignity of its language, and, not least, by its spiritual insight. It is a miracle of a poem.

A few words about the text presented here. Whitman's vision and his language were at their most powerful in the first edition of *Leaves of Grass*, published in 1855. As he grew older, his insight faded, and with it the vivacity of his words. Yet in each successive edition he kept tinkering with "Song of Myself" and the other early poems—adding, deleting, revising. And while certain of these revisions are excellent, most of them are disastrous. This has led to an affectionate frustration among some of Whitman's readers; we want the best of all possible editions.

For example, in a passionate and deservedly famous passage about music the text of the 1855 edition reads:

I hear the violincello or man's heart's complaint,
And hear the keyed cornet or else the echo of
sunset.

I hear the chorus . . . . it is a grand-opera . . . . this
indeed is music!

A tenor large and fresh as the creation fills me,
The orbic flex of his mouth is pouring and filling
me full.

I hear the trained soprano . . . . she convulses me
like the climax of my love-grip;
The orchestra whirls me wider than Uranus flies,
It wrenches unnamable ardors from my breast,
It throbs me to gulps of the farthest down horror,
It sails me . . . . I dab with bare feet . . . . they are
licked by the indolent waves,
I am exposed . . . . cut by bitter and poisoned hail,
Steeped amid honeyed morphine . . . . my
windpipe squeezed in the fakes of death,
Let up again to feel the puzzle of puzzles,
And that we call Being.

Whitman incorporated two brilliant revisions in the
second (1856) edition. There, line two reads:

I hear the keyed cornet, it glides quickly in
    through my ears, it shakes mad-sweet pangs
    through my belly and breast.

And line eight:

It wrenches such ardors from me, I did not know
    I possessed them

In 1860 he rewrote the transition from lines twelve to
thirteen in this way:

        my windpipe throttled in fakes of
  death,
At length let up again to feel

On the other hand, in the 1867 and later editions
Whitman ruined the sixth line by replacing its dan-
gerous sexuality with a phrase that is colorless, almost
meaningless, and a rhythm straight out of a hymnbook:

I hear the trained soprano (what work with hers
    is this?)

And he entirely deleted the weird and thrilling ninth
line.

If I were forced to choose between the original and any of the revised versions, I would certainly choose the former. But why give up anything that makes a great poem even greater? Why not keep the revisions that enliven and clarify, and disregard the ones that don't? The passage then sounds like this:

I hear the violincello or man's heart's complaint,
I hear the keyed cornet, it glides quickly in
    through my ears, it shakes mad-sweet pangs
    through my belly and breast.

I hear the chorus . . . . it is a grand-opera . . . . this
    indeed is music!

A tenor large and fresh as the creation fills me,
The orbic flex of his mouth is pouring and filling
    me full.

I hear the trained soprano . . . . she convulses me
    like the climax of my love-grip;
The orchestra whirls me wider than Uranus flies,
It wrenches such ardors from me, I did not know
    I possessed them,
It throbs me to gulps of the farthest down horror,

It sails me . . . . I dab with bare feet . . . . they are
  licked by the indolent waves,
I am exposed . . . . cut by bitter and poisoned hail,
Steeped amid honeyed morphine . . . . my wind-
  pipe throttled in fakes of death,
At length let up again to feel the puzzle of puzzles,
And that we call Being.

In this conflated version of "Song of Myself," I have
used the first edition as my main source, and I have ad-
opted any revision that seemed to be even a minor im-
provement. The section numbers, which first appeared
in 1867, may be useful in providing a more readily ap-
parent structure, but they are often arbitrary, and they
impede the uninterrupted flow of one stanza into the
next, over the whole expanse of the poem.

Although none of the poems had titles in the first
edition of Leaves of Grass, I have kept the 1876 edition's
"Song of Myself" because it is so familiar. Certainly
the poem embodies an outrageous egotism, an "I" so
shamelessly naked that even a bodhisattva can admire
it. But Whitman was also writing about selflessness,
about the Self beyond the self ("I and this mystery here
we stand"; "Apart from the pulling and hauling stands
what I am"), and it would have been just as appropriate
to call the poem "Song of My Self," in the Upanishads'
sense of the word:

Self is everywhere, shining forth from all beings, vaster than the vast, subtler than the most subtle, unreachable, yet nearer than breath, than heartbeat.

Egotism and selflessness: one contradiction among many. But the poem is large . . . . it contains and embraces multitudes.

SONG OF MYSELF

I celebrate myself,
And what I assume you shall assume,
For every atom belonging to me as good belongs to
 you.

I loafe and invite my soul,
I lean and loafe at my ease . . . . observing a spear of
 summer grass.

Houses and rooms are full of perfumes . . . . the
 shelves are crowded with perfumes,
I breathe the fragrance myself, and know it and like it,
The distillation would intoxicate me also, but I shall
 not let it.

The atmosphere is not a perfume . . . . it has no taste
 of the distillation . . . . it is odorless,
It is for my mouth forever . . . . I am in love with it,
I will go to the bank by the wood and become
 undisguised and naked,
I am mad for it to be in contact with me.

The smoke of my own breath,

Echoes, ripples, and buzzed whispers . . . . loveroot, silkthread, crotch and vine,

My respiration and inspiration . . . . the beating of my heart . . . . the passing of blood and air through my lungs,

The sniff of green leaves and dry leaves, and of the shore and darkcolored sea-rocks, and of hay in the barn,

The sound of the belched words of my voice . . . . words loosed to the eddies of the wind,

A few light kisses . . . . a few embraces . . . . a reaching around of arms,

The play of shine and shade on the trees as the supple boughs wag,

The delight alone or in the rush of the streets, or along the fields and hillsides,

The feeling of health . . . . the full-noon trill . . . . the song of me rising from bed and meeting the sun.

Have you reckoned a thousand acres much? Have you reckoned the earth much?

Have you practiced so long to learn to read?

Have you felt so proud to get at the meaning of poems?

Stop this day and night with me and you shall possess
    the origin of all poems,
You shall possess the good of the earth and sun . . . .
    there are millions of suns left,
You shall no longer take things at second or third
    hand . . . . nor look through the eyes of the dead
    . . . . nor feed on the spectres in books,
You shall not look through my eyes either, nor take
    things from me,
You shall listen to all sides and filter them from
    yourself.

I have heard what the talkers were talking . . . . the
    talk of the beginning and the end,
But I do not talk of the beginning or the end.

There was never any more inception than there is
    now,
Nor any more youth or age than there is now;
And will never be any more perfection than there is
    now,
Nor any more heaven or hell than there is now.

Urge and urge and urge,
Always the procreant urge of the world.

Out of the dimness opposite equals advance . . . .
    Always substance and increase, always sex,
Always a knit of identity . . . . always distinction . . . .
    always a breed of life.

To elaborate is no avail . . . . Learned and unlearned
    feel that it is so.

Sure as the most certain sure . . . . plumb in the
    uprights, well entretied, braced in the beams,
Stout as a horse, affectionate, haughty, electrical,
I and this mystery here we stand.

Clear and sweet is my soul . . . . and clear and sweet is
    all that is not my soul.

Lack one lacks both . . . . and the unseen is proved by
    the seen,
Till that becomes unseen and receives proof in its
    turn.

Showing the best and dividing it from the worst, age
    vexes age,
Knowing the perfect fitness and equanimity of things,
    while they discuss I am silent, and go bathe and
    admire myself.

Welcome is every organ and attribute of me, and of
    any man hearty and clean,
Not an inch nor a particle of an inch is vile, and none
    shall be less familiar than the rest.

I am satisfied . . . . I see, dance, laugh, sing;
As God comes a loving bedfellow and sleeps at my
    side all night and close on the peep of the day,
And leaves for me baskets covered with white towels
    bulging the house with their plenty,
Shall I postpone my acceptation and realization and
    scream at my eyes,
That they turn from gazing after and down the road,
And forthwith cipher and show me to a cent,
Exactly the contents of one, and exactly the contents
    of two, and which is ahead?

Trippers and askers surround me,
People I meet . . . . the effect upon me of my early
    life . . . . of the ward and city I live in . . . . of the
    nation,
The latest news . . . . discoveries, inventions, societies
    . . . . authors old and new,
My dinner, dress, associates, looks, business,
    compliments, dues,
The real or fancied indifference of some man or
    woman I love,

The sickness of one of my folks—or of myself . . . .
    or ill-doing . . . . or loss or lack of money . . . . or
    depressions or exaltations,
They come to me days and nights and go from me
    again,
But they are not the Me myself.

Apart from the pulling and hauling stands what I am,
Stands amused, complacent, compassionating, idle,
    unitary,
Looks down, is erect, bends an arm on an impalpable
    certain rest,
Looks with its sidecurved head curious what will
    come next,
Both in and out of the game, and watching and
    wondering at it.

Backward I see in my own days where I sweated
    through fog with linguists and contenders,
I have no mockings or arguments . . . . I witness and
    wait.

I believe in you my soul . . . . the other I am must not
    abase itself to you,
And you must not be abased to the other.

Loafe with me on the grass . . . . loose the stop from
    your throat,
Not words, not music or rhyme I want . . . . not
    custom or lecture, not even the best,
Only the lull I like, the hum of your valved voice.

I mind how we lay in June, such a transparent
    summer morning;
You settled your head athwart my hips and gently
    turned over upon me,
And parted the shirt from my bosom-bone, and
    plunged your tongue to my barestript heart,
And reached till you felt my beard, and reached till
    you held my feet.

Swiftly arose and spread around me the peace and
    knowledge that pass all the argument of the earth;
And I know that the hand of God is the elderhand of
    my own,
And I know that the spirit of God is the eldest brother
    of my own,
And that all the men ever born are also my brothers
    . . . . and the women my sisters and lovers, And
    that a kelson of the creation is love;
And limitless are leaves stiff or drooping in the fields,
And brown ants in the little wells beneath them,

And mossy scabs of the wormfence, and heaped
    stones, and elder and mullen and pokeweed.

A child said, What is the grass? fetching it to me with
    full hands;
How could I answer the child? . . . . I do not know
    what it is any more than he.

I guess it must be the flag of my disposition, out of
    hopeful green stuff woven.

Or I guess it is the handkerchief of the Lord,
A scented gift and remembrancer designedly
    dropped,
Bearing the owner's name someway in the corners,
    that we may see and remark, and say Whose?

Or I guess the grass is itself a child . . . . the produced
    babe of the vegetation.

Or I guess it is a uniform hieroglyphic,
And it means, Sprouting alike in broad zones and
    narrow zones,
Growing among black folks as among white,
Kanuck, Tuckahoe, Congressman, Cuff, I give them
    the same, I receive them the same.

And now it seems to me the beautiful uncut hair of
    graves.

Tenderly will I use you curling grass,
It may be you transpire from the breasts of young
    men,
It may be if I had known them I would have loved
    them;
It may be you are from old people, or from offspring
    taken soon out of their mothers' laps,
And here you are the mothers' laps.

This grass is very dark to be from the white heads of
    old mothers,
Darker than the colorless beards of old men,
Dark to come from under the faint red roofs of
    mouths.

O I perceive after all so many uttering tongues!
And I perceive they do not come from the roofs of
    mouths for nothing.

I wish I could translate the hints about the dead young
    men and women,
And the hints about old men and mothers, and the
    offspring taken soon out of their laps.

What do you think has become of the young and old
    men?
And what do you think has become of the women and
    children?

They are alive and well somewhere;
The smallest sprout shows there is really no death,
And if ever there was it led forward life, and does not
    wait at the end to arrest it,
And ceased the moment life appeared.

All goes onward and outward . . . . and nothing
    collapses,
And to die is different from what any one supposed,
    and luckier.

Has any one supposed it lucky to be born?
I hasten to inform him or her it is just as lucky to die,
    and I know it.

I pass death with the dying, and birth with the new-
    washed babe . . . . and am not contained between
    my hat and boots,
And peruse manifold objects, no two alike, and every
    one good,
The earth good, and the stars good, and their adjuncts
    all good.

I am not an earth nor an adjunct of an earth,
I am the mate and companion of people, all just as
    immortal and fathomless as myself;
They do not know how immortal, but I know.

Every kind for itself and its own . . . . for me mine
    male and female,
For me all that have been boys and that love women,
For me the man that is proud and feels how it stings
    to be slighted,
For me the sweetheart and the old maid . . . . for me
    mothers and the mothers of mothers,
For me lips that have smiled, eyes that have shed tears,
For me children and the begetters of children.

Who need be afraid of the merge?
Undrape . . . . you are not guilty to me, nor stale nor
    discarded,
I see through the broadcloth and gingham whether
    or no,
And am around, tenacious, acquisitive, tireless . . . .
    and can never be shaken away.

The little one sleeps in its cradle,
I lift the gauze and look a long time, and silently
    brush away flies with my hand.

The youngster and the redfaced girl turn aside up the
bushy hill,
I peeringly view them from the top.

The suicide sprawls on the bloody floor of the
bedroom,
I witness the corpse with its dabbled hair, I note
where the pistol has fallen.

The blab of the pave . . . . the tires of carts and sluff of
bootsoles and talk of the promenaders,
The heavy omnibus, the driver with his interrogating
thumb, the clank of the shod horses on the granite
floor,
The carnival of sleighs, the clinking and shouted jokes
and pelts of snowballs;
The hurrahs for popular favorites . . . . the fury of
roused mobs,
The flap of the curtained litter—the sick man inside,
borne to the hospital,
The meeting of enemies, the sudden oath, the blows
and fall,
The excited crowd—the policeman with his star
quickly working his passage to the centre of the
crowd;
The impassive stones that receive and return so many
echoes,

The souls moving along . . . . are they invisible while
    the least atom of the stones is visible?
What groans of overfed or half-starved who fall on
    the flags sunstruck or in fits,
What exclamations of women taken suddenly, who
    hurry home and give birth to babes,
What living and buried speech is always vibrating
    here . . . . what howls restrained by decorum,
Arrests of criminals, slights, adulterous offers made,
    acceptances, rejections with convex lips,
I mind them or the resonance of them . . . . I come
    and I depart.

The big doors of the country-barn stand open and
    ready,
The dried grass of the harvest-time loads the slow-
    drawn wagon,
The clear light plays on the brown gray and green
    intertinged,
The armfuls are packed to the sagging mow:
I am there . . . . I help . . . . I came stretched atop of
    the load,
I felt its soft jolts . . . . one leg reclined on the other,
I jump from the crossbeams, and seize the clover and
    timothy,
And roll head over heels, and tangle my hair full of
    wisps.

Alone far in the wilds and mountains I hunt,
Wandering amazed at my own lightness and glee,
In the late afternoon choosing a safe spot to pass the
    night,
Kindling a fire and broiling the freshkilled game,
Falling asleep on the gathered leaves, my dog and gun
    by my side.

The Yankee clipper is under her three skysails . . . .
    she cuts the sparkle and scud,
My eyes settle the land . . . . I bend at her prow or
    shout joyously from the deck.

The boatmen and clamdiggers arose early and
    stopped for me,
I tucked my trowser-ends in my boots and went and
    had a good time,
You should have been with us that day round the
    chowder-kettle.

I saw the marriage of the trapper in the open air in
    the far-west . . . . the bride was a red girl,
Her father and his friends sat near by crosslegged and
    dumbly smoking . . . . they had moccasins to their
    feet and large thick blankets hanging from their
    shoulders;
On a bank lounged the trapper . . . . he was dressed
    mostly in skins . . . . his luxuriant beard and curls

protected his neck. . . . he held his bride by the
hand,
She had long eyelashes . . . . her head was bare . . . .
her coarse straight locks descended upon her
voluptuous limbs and reached to her feet.

The runaway slave came to my house and stopped
outside,
I heard his motions crackling the twigs of the
woodpile,
Through the swung half-door of the kitchen I saw him
limpsy and weak,
And went where he sat on a log, and led him in and
assured him,
And brought water and filled a tub for his sweated
body and bruised feet,
And gave him a room that entered from my own, and
gave him some coarse clean clothes,
And remember perfectly well his revolving eyes and
his awkwardness,
And remember putting plasters on the galls of his
neck and ankles;
He staid with me a week before he was recuperated
and passed north,
I had him sit next me at table . . . . my firelock leaned
in the corner.

Twenty-eight young men bathe by the shore,
Twenty-eight young men, and all so friendly,
Twenty-eight years of womanly life, and all so
    lonesome.

She owns the fine house by the rise of the bank,
She hides handsome and richly drest aft the blinds of
    the window.

Which of the young men does she like the best?
Ah the homeliest of them is beautiful to her.

Where are you off to, lady? for I see you,
You splash in the water there, yet stay stock still in
    your room.

Dancing and laughing along the beach came the
    twenty-ninth bather,
The rest did not see her, but she saw them and loved
    them.

The beards of the young men glistened with wet, it
    ran from their long hair,
Little streams passed all over their bodies.

An unseen hand also passed over their bodies,
It descended tremblingly from their temples and ribs.

The young men float on their backs, their white
    bellies swell to the sun . . . . they do not ask who
    seizes fast to them,
They do not know who puffs and declines with
    pendant and bending arch,
They do not think whom they souse with spray.

The butcher-boy puts off his killing-clothes, or
    sharpens his knife at the stall in the market,
I loiter enjoying his repartee and his shuffle and
    breakdown.

Blacksmiths with grimed and hairy chests environ the
    anvil,
Each has his main-sledge . . . . they are all out . . . .
    there is a great heat in the fire.

From the cinder-strewed threshold I follow their
    movements,
The lithe sheer of their waists plays even with their
    massive arms,
Overhand the hammers roll—overhand so slow—
    overhand so sure,
They do not hasten, each man hits in his place.

The negro holds firmly the reins of his four horses
    . . . . the block swags underneath on its tied-over
    chain,

The negro that drives the huge dray of the stoneyard
        . . . . steady and tall he stands poised on one leg on
        the stringpiece,
His blue shirt exposes his ample neck and breast and
        loosens over his hipband,
His glance is calm and commanding . . . . he tosses
        the slouch of his hat away from his forehead,
The sun falls on his crispy hair and moustache . . . .
        falls on the black of his polish'd and perfect limbs.

I behold the picturesque giant and love him . . . . and I
        do not stop there,
I go with the team also.

In me the caresser of life wherever moving . . . .
        backward as well as forward slueing,
To niches aside and junior bending.

Oxen that rattle the yoke or halt in the shade, what is
        that you express in your eyes?
It seems to me more than all the print I have read in
        my life.

My tread scares the wood-drake and wood-duck on
        my distant and daylong ramble,
They rise together, they slowly circle around. . . . .
        I believe in those winged purposes,

And acknowledge the red yellow and white playing
    within me,
And consider the green and violet and the tufted
    crown intentional;
And do not call the tortoise unworthy because she is
    not something else,
And the mockingbird in the swamp never studied the
    gamut, yet trills pretty well to me,
And the look of the bay mare shames silliness out
    of me.

The wild gander leads his flock through the cool
    night,
Ya-honk! he says, and sounds it down to me like an
    invitation;
The pert may suppose it meaningless, but I listen
    closer,
I find its purpose and place up there toward the
    November sky.

The sharphoofed moose of the north, the cat on the
    housesill, the chickadee, the prairie-dog,
The litter of the grunting sow as they tug at her teats,
The brood of the turkeyhen, and she with her
    halfspread wings,
I see in them and myself the same old law.

The press of my foot to the earth springs a hundred
   affections,
They scorn the best I can do to relate them.

I am enamoured of growing outdoors,
Of men that live among cattle or taste of the ocean or
   woods,
Of the builders and steerers of ships, of the wielders
   of axes and mauls, of the drivers of horses,
I can eat and sleep with them week in and week out.

What is commonest and cheapest and nearest and
   easiest is Me,
Me going in for my chances, spending for vast
   returns,
Adorning myself to bestow myself on the first that
   will take me,
Not asking the sky to come down to my goodwill,
Scattering it freely forever.

The pure contralto sings in the organloft,
The carpenter dresses his plank . . . . the tongue of his
   foreplane whistles its wild ascending lisp,
The married and unmarried children ride home to
   their Thanksgiving dinner,
The pilot seizes the king-pin, he heaves down with a
   strong arm,

The mate stands braced in the whaleboat, lance and
	harpoon are ready,
The duck-shooter walks by silent and cautious
	stretches,
The deacons are ordained with crossed hands at the
	altar,
The spinning-girl retreats and advances to the hum of
	the big wheel,
The farmer stops by the bars of a Sunday and looks at
	the oats and rye,
The lunatic is carried at last to the asylum a
	confirmed case,
He will never sleep any more as he did in the cot in
	his mother's bedroom;
The jour printer with gray head and gaunt jaws works
	at his case,
He turns his quid of tobacco, his eyes get blurred
	with the manuscript;
The malformed limbs are tied to the anatomist's
	table,
What is removed drops horribly in a pail;
The quadroon girl is sold at the auction-stand
	. . . . the drunkard nods by the barroom stove,
The machinist rolls up his sleeves . . . . the policeman
	travels his beat . . . . the gate-keeper marks who
	pass,
The young fellow drives the express-wagon . . . .
	I love him though I do not know him;

The half-breed straps on his light boots to compete in
    the race,
The western turkey-shooting draws old and young
    . . . . some lean on their rifles, some sit on logs,
Out from the crowd steps the marksman and takes his
    position and levels his piece;
The groups of newly-come immigrants cover the
    wharf or levee,
The woollypates hoe in the sugarfield, the overseer
    views them from his saddle;
The bugle calls in the ballroom, the gentlemen run
    for their partners, the dancers bow to each other;
The youth lies awake in the cedar-roofed garret and
    harks to the musical rain,
The Wolverine sets traps on the creek that helps fill
    the Huron,
The reformer ascends the platform, he spouts with
    his mouth and nose,
The company returns from its excursion, the darkey
    brings up the rear and bears the well-riddled target,
The squaw wrapt in her yellow-hemmed cloth is
    offering moccasins and beadbags for sale,
The connoisseur peers along the exhibition-gallery
    with halfshut eyes bent sideways,
The deckhands make fast the steamboat, the plank is
    thrown for the shoregoing passengers,

The young sister holds out the skein, the elder sister
   winds it off in a ball and stops now and then for
   the knots,
The one-year wife is recovering and happy, a week
   ago she bore her first child,
The cleanhaired Yankee girl works with her sewing-
   machine or in the factory or mill,
The nine months' gone is in the parturition chamber,
   her faintness and pains are advancing;
The pavingman leans on his twohanded rammer—the
   reporter's lead flies swiftly over the notebook—
   the signpainter is lettering with red and gold,
The canal-boy trots on the towpath—the bookkeeper
   counts at his desk—the shoemaker waxes his
   thread,
The conductor beats time for the band and all the
   performers follow him,
The child is baptised—the convert is making his first
   professions,
The regatta is spread on the bay . . . . how the white
   sails sparkle!
The drover watches his drove, he sings out to them
   that would stray,
The pedlar sweats with his pack on his back—the
   purchaser higgles about the odd cent,
The camera and plate are prepared, the lady must sit
   for her daguerreotype,

The bride unrumples her white dress, the
    minutehand of the clock moves slowly,
The opium eater reclines with rigid head and just-
    opened lips,
The prostitute draggles her shawl, her bonnet bobs
    on her tipsy and pimpled neck,
The crowd laugh at her blackguard oaths, the men
    jeer and wink to each other,
(Miserable! I do not laugh at your oaths nor jeer you,)
The President holds a cabinet council, he is
    surrounded by the great secretaries,
On the piazza walk five friendly matrons with twined
    arms;
The crew of the fish-smack pack repeated layers of
    halibut in the hold,
The Missourian crosses the plains toting his wares and
    his cattle,
The fare-collector goes through the train—he gives
    notice by the jingling of loose change,
The floormen are laying the floor—the tinners are
    tinning the roof—the masons are calling for
    mortar,
In single file each shouldering his hod pass onward
    the laborers;
Seasons pursuing each other the indescribable crowd
    is gathered . . . . it is the Fourth of July . . . . what
    salutes of cannon and small arms!

Seasons pursuing each other the plougher ploughs
and the mower mows and the wintergrain falls in
the ground;
Off on the lakes the pikefisher watches and waits by
the hole in the frozen surface,
The stumps stand thick round the clearing, the
squatter strikes deep with his axe,
The flatboatmen make fast toward dusk near the
cottonwood or pekantrees,
The coon-seekers go now through the regions of
the Red river, or through those drained by the
Tennessee, or through those of the Arkansas,
The torches shine in the dark that hangs on the
Chattahoochee or Altamahaw;
Patriarchs sit at supper with sons and grandsons and
great grandsons around them,
In walls of adobe, in canvas tents, rest hunters and
trappers after their day's sport.
The city sleeps and the country sleeps,
The living sleep for their time . . . . the dead sleep for
their time,
The old husband sleeps by his wife and the young
husband sleeps by his wife;
And these one and all tend inward to me, and I tend
outward to them,
And such as it is to be of these more or less I am.

I am of old and young, of the foolish as much as the
    wise,
Regardless of others, ever regardful of others,
Maternal as well as paternal, a child as well as a man,
Stuffed with the stuff that is coarse, and stuffed with
    the stuff that is fine,
One of the great nation, the nation of many nations—
    the smallest the same and the largest the same,
A southerner soon as a northerner, a planter
    nonchalant and hospitable,
A Yankee bound my own way . . . . ready for trade
    . . . . my joints the limberest joints on earth and
    the sternest joints on earth,
A Kentuckian walking the vale of the Elkhorn in my
    deerskin leggings,
A boatman over the lakes or bays or along coasts . . . .
    a Hoosier, a Badger, a Buckeye,
A Louisianian or Georgian, a poke-easy from sandhills
    and pines,
At home on Canadian snowshoes or up in the bush, or
    with fishermen off Newfoundland,
At home in the fleet of iceboats, sailing with the rest
    and tacking,
At home on the hills of Vermont or in the woods of
    Maine or the Texan ranch,
Comrade of Californians . . . . comrade of free
    northwesterners, loving their big proportions,

Comrade of raftsmen and coalmen—comrade of all
    who shake hands and welcome to drink and meat;
A learner with the simplest, a teacher of the
    thoughtfulest,
A novice beginning experient of myriads of seasons,
Of every hue and trade and rank, of every caste and
    religion,
Not merely of the New World but of Africa Europe or
    Asia . . . . a wandering savage,
A farmer, mechanic, or artist . . . . a gentleman,
    sailor, lover or quaker,
A prisoner, fancy-man, rowdy, lawyer, physician or
    priest.

I resist anything better than my own diversity,
And breathe the air and leave plenty after me,
And am not stuck up, and am in my place.

The moth and the fisheggs are in their place,
The suns I see and the suns I cannot see are in their
    place,
The palpable is in its place and the impalpable is in its
    place.

These are the thoughts of all men in all ages and
    lands, they are not original with me,
If they are not yours as much as mine they are nothing
    or next to nothing,

If they do not enclose everything they are next to
     nothing,
If they are not the riddle and the untying of the riddle
     they are nothing,
If they are not just as close as they are distant they are
     nothing.

This is the grass that grows wherever the land is and
     the water is,
This is the common air that bathes the globe.

This is the breath of laws and songs and behavior,
This is the tasteless water of souls . . . . this is the true
     sustenance,
It is for the illiterate . . . . it is for the judges of the
     supreme court . . . . it is for the federal capitol and
     the state capitols,
It is for the admirable communes of literary men and
     composers and singers and lecturers and engineers
     and savans,
It is for the endless races of working people and
     farmers and seamen.

This is the trill of a thousand clear cornets and scream
     of the octave flute and strike of triangles.

I play not a march for victors only . . . . I play great
     marches for conquered and slain persons.

Have you heard that it was good to gain the day?
I also say it is good to fall . . . . battles are lost in the
    same spirit in which they are won.

I sound triumphal drums for the dead . . . . I fling
    through my embouchures the loudest and gayest
    music to them,
Vivas to those who have failed, and to those whose
    war-vessels sank in the sea, and those themselves
    who sank in the sea,
And to all generals that lost engagements, and all
    overcome heroes, and the numberless unknown
    heroes equal to the greatest heroes known.

This is the meal pleasantly set . . . . this is the meat
    and drink for natural hunger,
It is for the wicked just the same as the righteous . . . .
    I make appointments with all,
I will not have a single person slighted or left away,
The keptwoman and sponger and thief are hereby
    invited . . . . the heavy-lipped slave is invited . . . .
    the venerealee is invited,
There shall be no difference between them and the
    rest.

This is the press of a bashful hand . . . . this is the float
    and odor of hair,

This is the touch of my lips to yours . . . . this is the
    murmur of yearning,
This is the far-off depth and height reflecting my own
    face,
This is the thoughtful merge of myself and the outlet
    again.

Do you guess I have some intricate purpose?
Well I have . . . . for the April rain has, and the mica
    on the side of a rock has.

Do you take it I would astonish?
Does the daylight astonish? or the early redstart
    twittering through the woods?
Do I astonish more than they?

This hour I tell things in confidence,
I might not tell everybody but I will tell you.

Who goes there! hankering, gross, mystical, nude?
How is it I extract strength from the beef I eat?

What is a man anyhow? What am I? and what are you?
All I mark as my own you shall offset it with your own,
Else it were time lost listening to me.

I do not snivel that snivel the world over,
That months are vacuums and the ground but wallow
    and filth,
That life is a suck and a sell, and nothing remains at
    the end but threadbare crape and tears.

Whimpering and truckling fold with powders
    for invalids . . . . conformity goes to the
    fourth-removed,
I cock my hat as I please indoors or out.

Why should I pray? Why should I venerate and be
    ceremonious?

Having pried through the strata and analyzed to a hair,
    and counselled with doctors and calculated close,
I find no sweeter fat than sticks to my own bones.

In all people I see myself, none more and not one a
    barleycorn less,
And the good or bad I say of myself I say of them.

And I know I am solid and sound,
To me the converging objects of the universe
    perpetually flow,
All are written to me, and I must get what the writing
    means.

And I know I am deathless,
I know this orbit of mine cannot be swept by a
   carpenter's compass,
I know I shall not pass like a child's carlacue cut with
   a burnt stick at night.

I know I am august,
I do not trouble my spirit to vindicate itself or be
   understood,
I see that the elementary laws never apologize,
I reckon I behave no prouder than the level I plant my
   house by after all.

I exist as I am, that is enough,
If no other in the world be aware I sit content,
And if each and all be aware I sit content.

One world is aware, and by far the largest to me, and
   that is myself,
And whether I come to my own today or in ten
   thousand or ten million years,
I can cheerfully take it now, or with equal
   cheerfulness I can wait.

My foothold is tenoned and mortised in granite,
I laugh at what you call dissolution,
And I know the amplitude of time.

I am the poet of the body,
And I am the poet of the soul.

The pleasures of heaven are with me, and the pains of
    hell are with me,
The first I graft and increase upon myself . . . . the
    latter I translate into a new tongue.

I am the poet of the woman the same as the man,
And I say it is as great to be a woman as to be a man,
And I say there is nothing greater than the mother of
    men.

I chant a new chant of dilation or pride,
We have had ducking and deprecating about enough,
I show that size is only development.

Have you outstript the rest? Are you the President?
It is a trifle . . . . they will more than arrive there
    every one, and still pass on.

I am he that walks with the tender and growing night;
I call to the earth and sea half-held by the night.
Press close barebosomed night! Press close magnetic
    nourishing night!
Night of south winds! Night of the large few stars!
Still nodding night! Mad naked summer night!

Smile O voluptuous coolbreathed earth!
Earth of the slumbering and liquid trees!
Earth of departed sunset! Earth of the mountains
    misty-topt!
Earth of the vitreous pour of the full moon just tinged
    with blue!
Earth of shine and dark mottling the tide of the river!
Earth of the limpid gray of clouds brighter and
    clearer for my sake!
Far-swooping elbowed earth! Rich apple-blossomed
    earth!
Smile, for your lover comes!

Prodigal! you have given me love! . . . . therefore I to
    you give love!
O unspeakable passionate love!

Thruster holding me tight and that I hold tight!
We hurt each other as the bridegroom and the bride
    hurt each other.

You sea! I resign myself to you also . . . . I guess what
    you mean,
I behold from the beach your crooked inviting
    fingers,
I believe you refuse to go back without feeling of me;
We must have a turn together . . . . I undress . . . .
    hurry me out of sight of the land,

Cushion me soft . . . . rock me in billowy drowse,
Dash me with amorous wet . . . . I can repay you.

Sea of stretched ground-swells!
Sea breathing broad and convulsive breaths!
Sea of the brine of life! Sea of unshovelled and always-
    ready graves!
Howler and scooper of storms! Capricious and dainty
    sea!
I am integral with you . . . . I too am of one phase and
    of all phases.

Partaker of influx and efflux . . . . extoler of hate and
    conciliation,
Extoler of amies and those that sleep in each others'
    arms.

I am he attesting sympathy;
Shall I make my list of things in the house and skip the
    house that supports them?

I am the poet of commonsense and of the
    demonstrable and of immortality;
And am not the poet of goodness only . . . . I do not
    decline to be the poet of wickedness also.

Washes and razors for foofoos . . . . for me freckles
    and a bristling beard.

What blurt is it about virtue and about vice?
Evil propels me, and reform of evil propels me . . . .
    I stand indifferent,
My gait is no faultfinder's or rejecter's gait,
I moisten the roots of all that has grown.

Did you fear some scrofula out of the unflagging
    pregnancy?
Did you guess the celestial laws are yet to be worked
    over and rectified?

I step up to say that what we do is right and what we
    affirm is right . . . . and some is only the ore of
    right,
Witnesses of us . . . . one side a balance and the
    antipodal side a balance,
Soft doctrine as steady help as stable doctrine,
Thoughts and deeds of the present our rouse and
    early start.

This minute that comes to me over the past
    decillions,
There is no better than it and now.

What behaved well in the past or behaves well today
    is not such a wonder,
The wonder is always and always how there can be a
    mean man or an infidel.

Endless unfolding of words of ages!
And mine a word of the modern . . . . a word en
   masse.

A word of the faith that never balks,
One time as good as another time . . . . here or
   henceforward it is all the same to me.

A word of reality . . . . materialism first and last
   imbuing.

Hurrah for positive science! Long live exact
   demonstration!
Fetch stonecrop and mix it with cedar and branches
   of lilac;
This is the lexicographer or chemist . . . . this made a
   grammar of the old cartouches,
These mariners put the ship through dangerous
   unknown seas,
This is the geologist, and this works with the scalpel,
   and this is a mathematician.

Gentlemen I receive you, and attach and clasp hands
   with you,
The facts are useful and real . . . . they are not my
   dwelling . . . . I enter by them to an area of the
   dwelling.

I am less the reminder of property or qualities, and
    more the reminder of life,
And go on the square for my own sake and for others'
    sakes,
And make short account of neuters and geldings, and
    favor men and women fully equipped,
And beat the gong of revolt, and stop with fugitives
    and them that plot and conspire.

Walt Whitman, an American, one of the roughs, a
    kosmos,
Disorderly fleshy and sensual . . . . eating drinking
    and breeding,
No sentimentalist . . . . no stander above men and
    women or apart from them . . . . no more modest
    than immodest.

Unscrew the locks from the doors!
Unscrew the doors themselves from their jambs!

Whoever degrades another degrades me . . . . and
    whatever is done or said returns at last to me,
And whatever I do or say I also return.

Through me the afflatus surging and surging . . . .
    through me the current and index.

I speak the password primeval . . . . I give the sign of
    democracy;
By God! I will accept nothing which all cannot have
    their counterpart of on the same terms.

Through me many long dumb voices,
Voices of the interminable generations of slaves,
Voices of prostitutes and of deformed persons,
Voices of the diseased and despairing, and of thieves
    and dwarfs,
Voices of cycles of preparation and accretion,
And of the threads that connect the stars—and of
    wombs, and of the fatherstuff,
And of the rights of them the others are down upon,
Of the trivial and flat and foolish and despised,
Of fog in the air and beetles rolling balls of dung.

Through me forbidden voices,
Voices of sexes and lusts . . . . voices veiled, and I
    remove the veil,
Voices indecent by me clarified and transfigured.

I do not press my finger across my mouth,
I keep as delicate around the bowels as around the
    head and heart,
Copulation is no more rank to me than death is.

I believe in the flesh and the appetites,
Seeing hearing and feeling are miracles, and each part
    and tag of me is a miracle.

Divine am I inside and out, and I make holy whatever
    I touch or am touched from;
The scent of these arm-pits is aroma finer than prayer,
This head is more than churches or bibles or creeds.

If I worship one thing more than another it shall be
    the spread of my own body, or any part of it;
Translucent mould of me it shall be you,
Shaded ledges and rests, firm masculine coulter, it
    shall be you,
Whatever goes to the tilth of me it shall be you,
You my rich blood, your milky stream pale strippings
    of my life;
Breast that presses against other breasts it shall be
    you,
My brain it shall be your occult convolutions,
Root of washed sweet-flag, timorous pond-snipe,
    nest of guarded duplicate eggs, it shall be you,
Mixed tussled hay of head and beard and brawn it
    shall be you,
Trickling sap of maple, fibre of manly wheat, it shall
    be you;

Sun so generous it shall be you,
Vapors lighting and shading my face it shall be you,
You sweaty brooks and dews it shall be you,
Winds whose soft-tickling genitals rub against me it
    shall be you,
Broad muscular fields, branches of liveoak, loving
    lounger in my winding paths, it shall be you,
Hands I have taken, face I have kissed, mortal I have
    ever touched, it shall be you.

I dote on myself . . . . there is that lot of me, and all so
    luscious,
Each moment and whatever happens thrills me with
    joy.

I cannot tell how my ankles bend . . . . nor whence
    the cause of my faintest wish,
Nor the cause of the friendship I emit . . . . nor the
    cause of the friendship I take again.

To walk up my stoop is unaccountable . . . . I pause to
    consider if it really be,
That I eat and drink is spectacle enough for the great
    authors and schools,
A morning-glory at my window satisfies me more
    than the metaphysics of books.

To behold the daybreak!
The little light fades the immense and diaphanous
  shadows,
The air tastes good to my palate.

Hefts of the moving world at innocent gambols,
  silently rising, freshly exuding,
Scooting obliquely high and low.

Something I cannot see puts upward libidinous
  prongs,
Seas of bright juice suffuse heaven.

The earth by the sky staid with . . . . the daily close of
  their junction,
The heaved challenge from the east that moment over
  my head,
The mocking taunt, See then whether you shall be
  master!

Dazzling and tremendous how quick the sunrise
  would kill me,
If I could not now and always send sunrise out of me.

We also ascend dazzling and tremendous as the sun,
We found our own my soul in the calm and cool of
  the daybreak.

My voice goes after what my eyes cannot reach,
With the twirl of my tongue I encompass worlds and
   volumes of worlds.

Speech is the twin of my vision . . . . it is unequal to
   measure itself.

It provokes me forever,
It says sarcastically, Walt, you understand enough . . . .
   why don't you let it out then?

Come now I will not be tantalized . . . . you conceive
   too much of articulation.

Do you not know how the buds beneath are folded?
Waiting in gloom protected by frost,
The dirt receding before my prophetical screams,
I underlying causes to balance them at last,
My knowledge my live parts . . . . it keeping tally
   with the meaning of things,
Happiness . . . . which whoever hears me let him or
   her set out in search of this day.

My final merit I refuse you . . . . I refuse putting from
   me the best I am.

Encompass worlds but never try to encompass me,
I crowd your noisiest talk by looking toward you.

Writing and talk do not prove me,
I carry the plenum of proof and every thing else in my
    face,
With the hush of my lips I confound the topmost
    skeptic.

I think I will do nothing for a long time but listen,
And accrue what I hear into myself . . . . and let
    sounds contribute toward me.

I hear the bravuras of birds . . . . the bustle of growing
    wheat . . . . gossip of flames . . . . clack of sticks
    cooking my meals.

I hear the sound of the human voice . . . . a sound I
    love,
I hear all sounds as they are tuned to their uses . . . .
    sounds of the city and sounds out of the city . . . .
    sounds of the day and night;
Talkative young ones to those that like them . . . . the
    recitative of fish-pedlars and fruit-pedlars . . . . the
    loud laugh of workpeople at their meals,
The angry base of disjointed friendship . . . . the faint
    tones of the sick,
The judge with hands tight to the desk, his shaky lips
    pronouncing a death-sentence,
The heave'e'yo of stevedores unlading ships by the
    wharves . . . . the refrain of the anchor-lifters;

The ring of alarm-bells . . . . the cry of fire . . . . the
    whirr of swift-streaking engines and hose-carts
    with premonitory tinkles and colored lights,
The steam-whistle . . . . the solid roll of the train of
    approaching cars;
The slow-march played at night at the head of the
    association,
They go to guard some corpse . . . . the flag-tops are
    draped with black muslin.

I hear the violoncello or man's heart's complaint,
I hear the keyed cornet, it glides quickly in through
    my ears, it shakes mad-sweet pangs through my
    belly and breast.

I hear the chorus . . . . it is a grand-opera . . . . this
    indeed is music!

A tenor large and fresh as the creation fills me,
The orbic flex of his mouth is pouring and filling me
    full.

I hear the trained soprano . . . . she convulses me like
    the climax of my love-grip;
The orchestra whirls me wider than Uranus flies,
It wrenches such ardors from me, I did not know I
    possessed them,

It throbs me to gulps of the farthest down horror,
It sails me . . . . I dab with bare feet . . . . they are
    licked by the indolent waves,
I am exposed . . . . cut by bitter and poisoned hail,
Steeped amid honeyed morphine . . . . my windpipe
    throttled in fakes of death,
At length let up again to feel the puzzle of puzzles,
And that we call Being.

To be in any form, what is that?
If nothing lay more developed the quahaug and its
    callous shell were enough.

Mine is no callous shell,
I have instant conductors all over me whether I pass
    or stop,
They seize every object and lead it harmlessly
    through me.

I merely stir, press, feel with my fingers, and am
    happy,
To touch my person to some one else's is about as
    much as I can stand.

Is this then a touch? . . . . quivering me to a new
    identity,

Flames and ether making a rush for my veins,
Treacherous tip of me reaching and crowding to help
    them,
My flesh and blood playing out lightning, to strike
    what is hardly different from myself,
On all sides prurient provokers stiffening my limbs,
Straining the udder of my heart for its withheld drip,
Behaving licentious toward me, taking no denial,
Depriving me of my best as for a purpose,
Unbuttoning my clothes and holding me by the bare
    waist,
 Deluding my confusion with the calm of the sunlight
    and pasture fields,
Immodestly sliding the fellow-senses away,
They bribed to swap off with touch, and go and graze
    at the edges of me,
No consideration, no regard for my draining strength
    or my anger,
Fetching the rest of the herd around to enjoy them
    awhile,
Then all uniting to stand on a headland and worry me.

The sentries desert every other part of me,
They have left me helpless to a red marauder,
They all come to the headland to witness and assist
    against me.

I am given up by traitors;
I talk wildly . . . . I have lost my wits . . . . I and
    nobody else am the greatest traitor,
I went myself first to the headland . . . . my own
    hands carried me there.

You villain touch! what are you doing? . . . . my
    breath is tight in its throat;
Unclench your floodgates! you are too much for me.

Blind loving wrestling touch! Sheathed hooded
    sharptoothed touch!
Did it make you ache so leaving me?

Parting tracked by arriving . . . . perpetual payment
    of the perpetual loan,
Rich showering rain, and recompense richer
    afterward.

Sprouts take and accumulate . . . . stand by the curb
    prolific and vital,
Landscapes projected masculine full-sized and
    golden.

All truths wait in all things,
They neither hasten their own delivery nor resist it,
They do not need the obstetric forceps of the
    surgeon,

The insignificant is as big to me as any,
What is less or more than a touch?

Logic and sermons never convince,
The damp of the night drives deeper into my soul.

Only what proves itself to every man and woman
    is so,
Only what nobody denies is so.

A minute and a drop of me settle my brain;
I believe the soggy clods shall become lovers and
    lamps,
And a compend of compends is the meat of a man or
    woman,
And a summit and flower there is the feeling they
    have for each other,
And they are to branch boundlessly out of that lesson
    until it becomes omnific,
And until every one shall delight us, and we them.

I believe a leaf of grass is no less than the journeywork
    of the stars,
And the pismire is equally perfect, and a grain of
    sand, and the egg of the wren,
And the tree-toad is a chef-d'œuvre for the highest,
And the running blackberry would adorn the parlors
    of heaven,

And the narrowest hinge in my hands puts to scorn all
    machinery,
And the cow crunching with depressed head
    surpasses any statue,
And a mouse is miracle enough to stagger sextillions
    of infidels.

I find I incorporate gneiss and coal and long-threaded
    moss and fruits and grains and esculent roots,
And am stucco'd with quadrupeds and birds all over,
And have distanced what is behind me for good
    reasons,
And call any thing close again when I desire it.

In vain the speeding or shyness,
In vain the plutonic rocks send their old heat against
    my approach,
In vain the mastodon retreats beneath its own
    powdered bones,
In vain objects stand leagues off and assume manifold
    shapes,
In vain the ocean settling in hollows and the great
    monsters lying low,
In vain the buzzard houses herself with the sky,
In vain the snake slides through the creepers and logs,
In vain the elk takes to the inner passes of the woods,
In vain the razorbilled auk sails far north to
    Labrador,

I follow quickly . . . . I ascend to the nest in the fissure
of the cliff.

I think I could turn and live awhile with the animals
. . . . they are so placid and self-contained,
I stand and look at them long and long.

They do not sweat and whine about their condition,
They do not lie awake in the dark and weep for their
sins,
They do not make me sick discussing their duty to
God,
Not one is dissatisfied . . . . not one is demented with
the mania of owning things,
Not one kneels to another nor to his kind that lived
thousands of years ago,
Not one is respectable or unhappy over the whole
earth.

So they show their relations to me and I accept them;
They bring me tokens of myself . . . . they evince
them plainly in their possession.

I do not know where they got those tokens,
I must have passed that way untold times ago and
negligently dropt them,
Myself moving forward then and now and forever,

Gathering and showing more always and with velocity,
Infinite and omnigenous and the like of these among
     them;
Not too exclusive toward the reachers of my
     remembrancers,
Picking out here one that I love,
Choosing to go with him on brotherly terms.

A gigantic beauty of a stallion, fresh and responsive to
     my caresses,
Head high in the forehead and wide between the ears,
Limbs glossy and supple, tail dusting the ground,
Eyes well apart and full of sparkling wickedness . . . .
     ears finely cut and flexibly moving.

His nostrils dilate . . . . my heels embrace him . . . .
     his well built limbs tremble with pleasure . . . . we
     speed around and return.

I but use you a moment and then I resign you stallion
     . . . . and do not need your paces, and outgallop
     them,
And myself as I stand or sit pass faster than you.

Swift wind! Space! My Soul! Now I know it is true
     what I guessed at;

What I guessed when I loafed on the grass,
What I guessed while I lay alone in my bed . . . . and
again as I walked the beach under the paling stars
of the morning.

My ties and ballasts leave me . . . . I travel . . . . I sail
. . . . my elbows rest in the sea-gaps,
I skirt the sierras . . . . my palms cover continents,
I am afoot with my vision.

By the city's quadrangular houses . . . . in log-huts, or
camping with lumbermen,
Along the ruts of the turnpike . . . . along the dry
gulch and rivulet bed,
Hoeing my onion-patch, and rows of carrots and
parsnips . . . . crossing savannas . . . . trailing in
forests,
Prospecting . . . . gold-digging . . . . girdling the trees
of a new purchase,
Scorched ankle-deep by the hot sand . . . . hauling my
boat down the shallow river;
Where the panther walks to and fro on a limb
overhead . . . . where the buck turns furiously at
the hunter,
Where the rattlesnake suns his flabby length on a rock
. . . . where the otter is feeding on fish,
Where the alligator in his tough pimples sleeps by the
bayou,

Where the black bear is searching for roots or honey
    . . . . where the beaver pats the mud with his
    paddle-tail;
Over the growing sugar . . . . over the cottonplant . . . .
    over the rice in its low moist field;
Over the sharp-peaked farmhouse with its scalloped
    scum and slender shoots from the gutters;
Over the western persimmon . . . . over the
    longleaved corn and the delicate blueflowered flax;
Over the white and brown buckwheat, a hummer and
    a buzzer there with the rest,
Over the dusky green of the rye as it ripples and
    shades in the breeze;
Scaling mountains . . . . pulling myself cautiously up
    . . . . holding on by low scragged limbs,
Walking the path worn in the grass and beat through
    the leaves of the brush;
Where the quail is whistling betwixt the woods and
    the wheatlot,
Where the bat flies in the July eve . . . . where the
    great goldbug drops through the dark;
Where the flails keep time on the barn floor,
Where the brook puts out of the roots of the old tree
    and flows to the meadow,
Where cattle stand and shake away flies with the
    tremulous shuddering of their hides,

Where the cheese-cloth hangs in the kitchen, and
    andirons straddle the hearth-slab, and cobwebs fall
    in festoons from the rafters;
Where triphammers crash . . . . where the press is
    whirling its cylinders;
Wherever the human heart beats with terrible throes
    out of its ribs;
Where the pear-shaped balloon is floating aloft . . . .
    floating in it myself and looking composedly down;
Where the life-car is drawn on the slipnoose . . . .
    where the heat hatches pale-green eggs in the
    dented sand,
Where the she-whale swims with her calves and
    never forsakes them,
Where the steamship trails hindways its long pennant
    of smoke,
Where the ground-shark's fin cuts like a black chip
    out of the water,
Where the half-burned brig is riding on unknown
    currents,
Where shells grow to her slimy deck, and the dead
    are corrupting below;
Where the striped and starred flag is borne at the
    head of the regiments;
Approaching Manhattan, up by the long-stretching
    island,

Under Niagara, the cataract falling like a veil over my
 countenance;
Upon a door-step . . . . upon the horse-block of hard
 wood outside,
Upon the race-course, or enjoying picnics or jigs or a
 good game of baseball,
At he-festivals with blackguard jibes and ironical
 license and bull-dances and drinking and laughter,
At the cider-mill, tasting the sweet of the brown
 sqush . . . . sucking the juice through a straw,
At apple-peelings, wanting kisses for all the red fruit
 I find,
At musters and beach-parties and friendly bees and
 huskings and house-raisings;
Where the mockingbird sounds his delicious gurgles,
 and cackles and screams and weeps,
Where the hay-rick stands in the barnyard, and the
 dry-stalks are scattered, and the brood cow waits
 in the hovel,
Where the bull advances to do his masculine work,
 and the stud to the mare, and the cock is treading
 the hen,
Where the heifers browse, and the geese nip their
 food with short jerks;
Where the sundown shadows lengthen over the
 limitless and lonesome prairie,
Where the herds of buffalo make a crawling spread of
 the square miles far and near;

Where the hummingbird shimmers . . . . where the
    neck of the longlived swan is curving and winding;
Where the laughing-gull scoots by the slappy shore
    and laughs her near-human laugh;
Where beehives range on a gray bench in the garden
    half-hid by the high weeds;
Where the band-necked partridges roost in a ring on
    the ground with their heads out;
Where burial coaches enter the arched gates of a
    cemetery;
Where winter wolves bark amid wastes of snow and
    icicled trees;
Where the yellow-crowned heron comes to the edge
    of the marsh at night and feeds upon small crabs;
Where the splash of swimmers and divers cools the
    warm noon;
Where the katydid works her chromatic reed on the
    walnut-tree over the well;
Through patches of citrons and cucumbers with
    silver-wired leaves,
Through the salt-lick or orange glade . . . . or under
    conical firs;
Through the gymnasium . . . . through the curtained
    saloon . . . . through the office or public hall;
Pleased with the native and pleased with the foreign
    . . . . pleased with the new and old,
Pleased with women, the homely as well as the
    handsome,

Pleased with the quakeress as she puts off her bonnet
and talks melodiously,
Pleased with the primitive tunes of the choir of the
whitewashed church,
Pleased with the earnest words of the sweating
Methodist preacher, or any preacher . . . . looking
seriously at the camp-meeting;
Looking in at the shop-windows of Broadway the
whole forenoon . . . . flatting the flesh of my nose
on the thick plate-glass,
Wandering the same afternoon with my face turned
up to the clouds;
My right and left arms round the sides of two friends
and I in the middle;
Coming home with the bearded and dark-cheeked
bush-boy . . . . riding behind him at the drape of
the day;
Far from the settlements studying the print of
animals' feet, or the moccasin print;
By the cot in the hospital reaching lemonade to a
feverish patient,
By the coffined corpse when all is still, examining
with a candle;
Voyaging to every port to dicker and adventure;
Hurrying with the modern crowd, as eager and fickle
as any,
Hot toward one I hate, ready in my madness to knife
him;

Solitary at midnight in my back yard, my thoughts
    gone from me a long while,
Walking the old hills of Judea with the beautiful
    gentle god by my side;
Speeding through space . . . . speeding through
    heaven and the stars,
Speeding amid the seen satellites and the broad ring
    and the diameter of eighty thousand miles,
Speeding with tailed meteors . . . . throwing fire-balls
    like the rest,
Carrying the crescent child that carries its own full
    mother in its belly;
Storming enjoying planning loving cautioning,
Backing and filling, appearing and disappearing,
I tread day and night such roads.

I visit the orchards of God and look at the spheric
    product,
And look at quintillions ripened, and look at
    quintillions green.

I fly the flight of the fluid and swallowing soul,
My course runs below the soundings of plummets.

I help myself to material and immaterial,
No guard can shut me off, no law can prevent me.

I anchor my ship for a little while only,
My messengers continually cruise away or bring their
    returns to me.

I go hunting polar furs and the seal . . . . leaping
    chasms with a pike-pointed staff . . . . clinging to
    topples of brittle and blue.

I ascend to the foretruck . . . . I take my place late at
    night in the crow's nest . . . . we sail through the
    arctic sea . . . . it is plenty light enough,
Through the clear atmosphere I stretch around on the
    wonderful beauty,
The enormous masses of ice pass me and I pass them
    . . . . the scenery is plain in all directions,
The white-topped mountains point up in the distance
    . . . . I fling out my fancies toward them;
We are approaching some great battlefield in which
    we are soon to be engaged,
We pass the colossal outposts of the encampments
    . . . . we pass with still feet and caution;
Or we are entering by the suburbs some vast and
    ruined city . . . . the blocks and fallen architecture
    more than all the living cities of the globe.

I am a free companion . . . . I bivouac by invading
    watchfires.

I turn the bridegroom out of bed and stay with the
    bride myself,
And tighten her all night to my thighs and lips.

My voice is the wife's voice, the screech by the rail of
    the stairs,
They fetch my man's body up dripping and drowned.

I understand the large hearts of heroes,
The courage of present times and all times;
How the skipper saw the crowded and rudderless
    wreck of the steamship, and death chasing it up
    and down the storm,
How he knuckled tight and gave not back one inch,
    and was faithful of days and faithful of nights,
And chalked in large letters on a board, Be of good
    cheer, We will not desert you;
How he saved the drifting company at last,
How the lank loose-gowned women looked when
    boated from the side of their prepared graves,
How the silent old-faced infants, and the lifted sick,
    and the sharp-lipped unshaved men;
All this I swallow and it tastes good . . . . I like it well,
    it becomes mine,
I am the man . . . . I suffered . . . . I was there.

The disdain and calmness of martyrs,
The mother condemned for a witch and burnt with
  dry wood, and her children gazing on;
The hounded slave that flags in the race and leans by
  the fence, blowing and covered with sweat,
The twinges that sting like needles his legs and neck,
The murderous buckshot and the bullets,
All these I feel or am.

I am the hounded slave . . . . I wince at the bite of the
  dogs,
Hell and despair are upon me . . . . crack and again
  crack the marksmen,
I clutch the rails of the fence . . . . my gore dribs
  thinned with the ooze of my skin,
I fall on the weeds and stones,
The riders spur their unwilling horses and haul close,
They taunt my dizzy ears . . . . they beat me violently
  over the head with their whip-stocks.

Agonies are one of my changes of garments;
I do not ask the wounded person how he feels . . . .
  I myself become the wounded person,
My hurt turns livid upon me as I lean on a cane and
  observe.

I am the mashed fireman with breastbone broken . . . .
  tumbling walls buried me in their debris,

Heat and smoke I inspired . . . . I heard the yelling
    shouts of my comrades,
I heard the distant click of their picks and shovels;
They have cleared the beams away . . . . they tenderly
    lift me forth.

I lie in the night air in my red shirt . . . . the pervading
    hush is for my sake,
Painless after all I lie, exhausted but not so unhappy,
White and beautiful are the faces around me . . . . the
    heads are bared of their fire-caps,
The kneeling crowd fades with the light of the
    torches.

Distant and dead resuscitate,
They show as the dial or move as the hands of me . . . .
    and I am the clock myself.

I am an old artillerist, and tell of my fort's
    bombardment . . . . and am there again.

Again the reveille of drummers . . . . again the
    attacking cannon and mortars and howitzers,
Again the attacked send their cannon responsive.

I take part . . . . I see and hear the whole,
The cries and curses and roar . . . . the plaudits for
    well aimed shots,

The ambulanza slowly passing and trailing its red
    drip,
Workmen searching after damages, making
    indispensable repairs,
The fall of grenades through the rent roof . . . . the
    fan-shaped explosion,
The whizz of limbs heads stone wood and iron high in
    the air.

Again gurgles the mouth of my dying general . . . . he
    furiously waves with his hand,
He gasps through the clot . . . . Mind not me . . . .
    mind . . . . the entrenchments.

I tell not the fall of Alamo . . . . not one escaped to
    tell the fall of Alamo,
The hundred and fifty are dumb yet at Alamo.

Hear now the tale of a jetblack sunrise,
Hear of the murder in cold blood of four hundred and
    twelve young men.

Retreating they had formed in a hollow square with
    their baggage for breastworks,
Nine hundred lives out of the surrounding enemy's
    nine times their number was the price they took in
    advance,

Their colonel was wounded and their ammunition
    gone,
They treated for an honorable capitulation, received
    writing and seal, gave up their arms, and marched
    back prisoners of war.

They were the glory of the race of rangers,
Matchless with a horse, a rifle, a song, a supper or a
    courtship,
Large, turbulent, brave, handsome, generous, proud
    and affectionate,
Bearded, sunburnt, dressed in the free costume of
    hunters,
Not a single one over thirty years of age.

The second Sunday morning they were brought out
    in squads and massacred . . . . it was beautiful early
    summer,
The work commenced about five o'clock and was
    over by eight.

None obeyed the command to kneel,
Some made a mad and helpless rush . . . . some stood
    stark and straight,
A few fell at once, shot in the temple or heart . . . .
    the living and dead lay together,

The maimed and mangled dug in the dirt . . . . the
   new-comers saw them there;
Some half-killed attempted to crawl away,
These were dispatched with bayonets or battered
   with the blunts of muskets;
A youth not seventeen years old seized his assassin till
   two more came to release him,
The three were all torn, and covered with the boy's
   blood.

At eleven o'clock began the burning of the bodies;
And that is the tale of the murder of the four hundred
   and twelve young men,
And that was a jetblack sunrise.

Did you read in the seabooks of the oldfashioned
   frigate-fight?
Did you learn who won by the light of the moon and
   stars?

Our foe was no skulk in his ship, I tell you,
His was the English pluck, and there is no tougher or
   truer, and never was, and never will be;
Along the lowered eve he came, horribly raking us.

We closed with him . . . . the yards entangled . . . .
   the cannon touched,
My captain lashed fast with his own hands.

We had received some eighteen-pound shots under
    the water,
 On our lower-gun-deck two large pieces had burst
    at the first fire, killing all around and blowing up
    overhead.

Ten o'clock at night, and the full moon shining
    and the leaks on the gain, and five feet of water
    reported,
The master-at-arms loosing the prisoners confined
    in the after-hold to give them a chance for
    themselves.

The transit to and from the magazine was now
    stopped by the sentinels,
They saw so many strange faces they did not know
    whom to trust.

Our frigate was afire . . . . the other asked if we
    demanded quarter? if our colors were struck and
    the fighting done?

I laughed content when I heard the voice of my little
    captain,
We have not struck, he composedly cried, We have
    just begun our part of the fighting.

Only three guns were in use,
One was directed by the captain himself against the
    enemy's mainmast,
Two well-served with grape and canister silenced his
    musketry and cleared his decks.

The tops alone seconded the fire of this little battery,
    especially the maintop,
They all held out bravely during the whole of the
    action.

Not a moment's cease,
The leaks gained fast on the pumps . . . . the fire eats
    toward the powder-magazine,
One of the pumps was shot away . . . . it was
    generally thought we were sinking.

Serene stood the little captain,
He was not hurried . . . . his voice was neither high
    nor low,
His eyes gave more light to us than our
    battle-lanterns.
Toward twelve at night, there in the beams of the
    moon they surrendered to us.

Stretched and still lay the midnight,
Two great hulls motionless on the breast of the
    darkness,

Our vessel riddled and slowly sinking . . . .
    preparations to pass to the one we had conquered,
The captain on the quarter deck coldly giving his
    orders through a countenance white as a sheet,
Near by the corpse of the child that served in the cabin,
The dead face of an old salt with long white hair and
    carefully curled whiskers,
The flames spite of all that could be done flickering
    aloft and below,
The husky voices of the two or three officers yet fit
    for duty,
Formless stacks of bodies and bodies by themselves
    . . . . dabs of flesh upon the masts and spars,
The cut of cordage and dangle of rigging . . . . the
    slight shock of the soothe of waves,
Black and impassive guns, and litter of powder-
    parcels, and the strong scent,
Delicate sniffs of the seabreeze . . . . smells of sedgy
    grass and fields by the shore . . . . death-messages
    given in charge to survivors,
The hiss of the surgeon's knife and the gnawing teeth
    of his saw,
The wheeze, the cluck, the swash of falling blood
    . . . . the short wild scream, the long dull tapering
    groan,
These so . . . . these irretrievable.

O Christ! My fit is mastering me!

What the rebel said gaily adjusting his throat to the
    rope-noose,

What the savage at the stump, his eye-sockets empty,
    his mouth spirting whoops and defiance,

What stills the traveler come to the vault at Mount
    Vernon,

What sobers the Brooklyn boy as he looks down the
    shores of the Wallabout and remembers the prison
    ships,

What burnt the gums of the redcoat at Saratoga when
    he surrendered his brigades,

These become mine and me every one, and they are
    but little,

I become as much more as I like.

I embody all presences outlawed or suffering,

And see myself in prison shaped like another man,

And feel the dull unintermitted pain.

For me the keepers of convicts shoulder their
    carbines and keep watch,

It is I let out in the morning and barred at night.

Not a mutineer walks handcuffed to the jail, but I am
    handcuffed to him and walk by his side,

I am less the jolly one there, and more the silent one
    with sweat on my twitching lips.

Not a youngster is taken for larceny, but I go up too
    and am tried and sentenced.

Not a cholera patient lies at the last gasp, but I also lie
    at the last gasp,
My face is ash-colored, my sinews gnarl . . . . away
    from me people retreat.

Askers embody themselves in me, and I am embodied
    in them,
I project my hat and sit shamefaced and beg.

I rise extatic through all, and sweep with the true
    gravitation,
The whirling and whirling is elemental within me.

Somehow I have been stunned. Stand back!
Give me a little time beyond my cuffed head and
    slumbers and dreams and gaping,
I discover myself on a verge of the usual mistake.

That I could forget the mockers and insults!
That I could forget the trickling tears and the blows
    of the bludgeons and hammers!
That I could look with a separate look on my own
    crucifixion and bloody crowning!

I remember . . . . I resume the overstaid fraction,
The grave of rock multiplies what has been confided
    to it . . . . or to any graves,
The corpses rise . . . . the gashes heal . . . . the
    fastenings roll away.

I troop forth replenished with supreme power, one of
    an average unending procession,
We walk the roads of Ohio and Massachusetts and
    Virginia and Wisconsin and New York and New
    Orleans and Texas and Montreal and San Francisco
    and Charleston and Savannah and Mexico,
Inland and by the seacoast and boundary lines . . . .
    and we pass the boundary lines.

Our swift ordinances are on their way over the whole
    earth,
The blossoms we wear in our hats are the growth of
    two thousand years.

Eleves I salute you,
I see the approach of your numberless gangs I
    see you understand yourselves and me,
And know that they who have eyes are divine, and the
    blind and lame are equally divine,
And that my steps drag behind yours yet go before
    them,

And are aware how I am with you no more than I am
    with everybody.

The friendly and flowing savage . . . . Who is he?
Is he waiting for civilization or past it and mastering it?

Is he some southwesterner raised outdoors? Is he
    Canadian?
Is he from the Mississippi country? or from Iowa,
    Oregon or California? or from the mountains? or
    prairie life or bush-life? or from the sea?

Wherever he goes men and women accept and desire
    him,
They desire he should like them and touch them and
    speak to them and stay with them.

Behaviour lawless as snow-flakes . . . . words simple
    as grass . . . . uncombed head and laughter and
    naiveté;
Slowstepping feet and the common features, and the
    common modes and emanations,
They descend in new forms from the tips of his
    fingers,
They are wafted with the odor of his body or breath
    . . . . they fly out of the glance of his eyes.

Flaunt of the sunshine I need not your bask . . . . lie
    over,
You light surfaces only . . . . I force the surfaces and
    the depths also.

Earth! you seem to look for something at my hands,
Say old topknot! what do you want?

Man or woman! I might tell how I like you, but
    cannot,
And might tell what it is in me and what it is in you,
    but cannot,
And might tell the pinings I have . . . . the pulse of my
    nights and days.

Behold I do not give lectures or a little charity,
What I give I give out of myself.

You there, impotent, loose in the knees, open your
    scarfed chops till I blow grit within you,
Spread your palms and lift the flaps of your pockets,
I am not to be denied . . . . I compel . . . . I have stores
    plenty and to spare,
And any thing I have I bestow.

I do not ask who you are . . . . that is not important
    to me,

You can do nothing and be nothing but what I will
    infold you.

To a drudge of the cottonfields or emptier of privies
    I lean . . . . on his right cheek I put the family kiss,
And in my soul I swear I never will deny him.

On women fit for conception I start bigger and
    nimbler babes,
This day I am jetting the stuff of far more arrogant
    republics.

To any one dying . . . . thither I speed and twist the
    knob of the door,
Turn the bedclothes toward the foot of the bed,
Let the physician and the priest go home.

I seize the descending man . . . . I raise him with
    resistless will.

O despairer, here is my neck,
By God! you shall not go down! Hang your whole
    weight upon me.

I dilate you with tremendous breath . . . . I buoy
    you up;

Every room of the house do I fill with an armed force
    . . . . lovers of me, bafflers of graves:
Sleep! I and they keep guard all night;
Not doubt, not decease shall dare to lay finger upon
    you,
I have embraced you, and henceforth possess you to
    myself,
And when you rise in the morning you will find what
    I tell you is so.

I am he bringing help for the sick as they pant on
    their backs,
 And for strong upright men I bring yet more needed
    help.

I heard what was said of the universe,
Heard it and heard of several thousand years;
It is middling well as far as it goes . . . . but is that all?

Magnifying and applying come I,
Outbidding at the start the old cautious hucksters,
The most they offer for mankind and eternity less
    than a spirt of my own seminal wet,
Taking myself the exact dimensions of Jehovah and
    laying them away,
Lithographing Kronos and Zeus his son, and Hercules
    his grandson,

Buying drafts of Osiris and Isis and Belus and Brahma and Buddha,

In my portfolio placing Manito loose, and Allah on a leaf, and the crucifix engraved,

With Odin, and the hideous-faced Mexitli, and all idols and images,

Taking them all for what they are worth, and not a cent more,

Admitting they were alive and did the work of their day,

Admitting they bore mites as for unfledged birds who have now to rise and fly and sing for themselves,

Accepting the rough deific sketches to fill out better in myself . . . . bestowing them freely on each man and woman I see,

Discovering as much or more in a framer framing a house,

Putting higher claims for him there with his rolled-up sleeves, driving the mallet and chisel;

Not objecting to special revelations . . . . considering a curl of smoke or a hair on the back of my hand as curious as any revelation;

Those ahold of fire-engines and hook-and-ladder ropes more to me than the gods of the antique wars,

Minding their voices peal through the crash of destruction,

Their brawny limbs passing safe over charred laths
    . . . . their white foreheads whole and unhurt out
    of the flames;
By the mechanic's wife with her babe at her nipple
    interceding for every person born;
Three scythes at harvest whizzing in a row from three
    lusty angels with shirts bagged out at their waists;
The snag-toothed hostler with red hair redeeming
    sins past and to come,
Selling all he possesses and traveling on foot to fee
    lawyers for his brother and sit by him while he is
    tried for forgery:
What was strewn in the amplest strewing the square
    rod about me, and not filling the square rod then;
The bull and the bug never worshipped half enough,
Dung and dirt more admirable than was dreamed,
The supernatural of no account . . . . myself waiting
    my time to be one of the supremes,
The day getting ready for me when I shall do as much
    good as the best, and be as prodigious,
Guessing when I am it will not tickle me much to
    receive puffs out of pulpit or print;
By my life-lumps! becoming already a creator!
Putting myself here and now to the ambushed womb
    of the shadows!

. . . . A call in the midst of the crowd,
My own voice, orotund sweeping and final.

Come my children,
Come my boys and girls, and my women and
household and intimates,
Now the performer launches his nerve . . . . he has
passed his prelude on the reeds within.

Easily written loosefingered chords! I feel the thrum
of their climax and close.

My head slues round on my neck,
Music rolls, but not from the organ . . . . folks are
around me, but they are no household of mine.

Ever the hard and unsunk ground,
Ever the eaters and drinkers . . . . ever the upward
and downward sun . . . . ever the air and the
ceaseless tides,
Ever myself and my neighbors, refreshing and wicked
and real,
Ever the old inexplicable query . . . . ever that
thorned thumb—that breath of itches and thirsts,
Ever the vexer's hoot! hoot! till we find where the sly
one hides and bring him forth;
Ever love . . . . ever the sobbing liquid of life,
Ever the bandage under the chin . . . . ever the
tressels of death.

Here and there with dimes on the eyes walking,
To feed the greed of the belly the brains liberally
    spooning,
Tickets buying or taking or selling, but in to the feast
    never once going;
Many sweating and ploughing and thrashing, and then
    the chaff for payment receiving,
A few idly owning, and they the wheat continually
    claiming.

This is the city . . . . and I am one of the citizens;
Whatever interests the rest interests me . . . . politics,
    churches, newspapers, schools,
Benevolent societies, improvements, banks, tariffs,
    steamships, factories, markets,
Stocks and stores and real estate and personal estate.

The little plentiful manikins skipping around in
    collars and tailed coats . . . . I am aware who they
    are . . . . and that they are not worms or fleas,
I acknowledge the duplicates of myself under all the
    scrape-lipped and pipe-legged concealments.

The weakest and shallowest is deathless with me,
What I do and say the same waits for them,
Every thought that flounders in me the same
    flounders in them.

I know perfectly well my own egotism,

And know my omniverous words, and cannot say any less,

And would fetch you whoever you are flush with myself.

My words are words of a questioning, and to indicate reality;

This printed and bound book . . . . but the printer and the printing-office boy?

The marriage estate and settlement . . . . but the body and mind of the bridegroom? also those of the bride?

The panorama of the sea . . . . but the sea itself?

The well-taken photographs . . . . but your wife or friend close and solid in your arms?

The fleet of ships of the line and all the modern improvements . . . . but the craft and pluck of the admiral?

The dishes and fare and furniture . . . . but the host and hostess, and the look out of their eyes?

The sky up there . . . . yet here or next door or across the way?

The saints and sages in history . . . . but you yourself?

Sermons and creeds and theology . . . . but the human brain, and what is called reason, and what is called love, and what is called life?

I do not despise you priests;
My faith is the greatest of faiths and the least of faiths,
Enclosing all worship ancient and modern, and all
between ancient and modern,
Believing I shall come again upon the earth after five
thousand years,
Waiting responses from oracles . . . . honoring the
gods . . . . saluting the sun,
Making a fetish of the first rock or stump . . . .
powowing with sticks in the circle of obis,
Helping the lama or brahmin as he trims the lamps of
the idols,
Dancing yet through the streets in a phallic procession
. . . . rapt and austere in the woods, a gymnosophist,
Drinking mead from the skull-cup . . . . to shasta and
vedas admirant . . . . minding the koran,
Walking the teokallis, spotted with gore from the
stone and knife—beating the serpent-skin drum;
Accepting the gospels, accepting him that was
crucified, knowing assuredly that he is divine,
To the mass kneeling—to the puritan's prayer
rising—sitting patiently in a pew,
Ranting and frothing in my insane crisis—waiting
dead-like till my spirit arouses me;
Looking forth on pavement and land, and outside of
pavement and land,
Belonging to the winders of the circuit of circuits.

One of that centripetal and centrifugal gang,
I turn and talk like a man leaving charges before a
   journey.

Down-hearted doubters, dull and excluded,
Frivolous sullen moping angry affected disheartened
   atheistical,
I know every one of you, I know the sea of torment,
   despair and unbelief.

How the flukes splash!
How they contort rapid as lightning, with spasms and
   spouts of blood!

Be at peace bloody flukes of doubters and sullen
   mopers,
I take my place among you as much as among any;
The past is the push of you and me and all precisely
   the same,
And the night is for you and me and all,
And what is yet untried and afterward is for you and
   me and all.

I do not know what is untried and afterward,
But I know it is sure and alive and sufficient.

Each who passes is considered, and each who stops is
   considered, and not a single one can it fail.

It cannot fail the young man who died and was buried,
Nor the young woman who died and was put by his
    side,
Nor the little child that peeped in at the door and
    then drew back and was never seen again,
Nor the old man who has lived without purpose, and
    feels it with bitterness worse than gall,
Nor him in the poorhouse tubercled by rum and the
    bad disorder,
Nor the numberless slaughtered and wrecked
    . . . . nor the brutish koboo, called the ordure of
    humanity,
Nor the sacs merely floating with open mouths for
    food to slip in,
Nor any thing in the earth, or down in the oldest
    graves of the earth,
Nor any thing in the myriads of spheres, nor one of
    the myriads of myriads that inhabit them,
Nor the present, nor the least wisp that is known.

It is time to explain myself . . . . let us stand up.

What is known I strip away . . . . I launch all men and
    women forward with me into the unknown.

The clock indicates the moment . . . . but what does
    eternity indicate?

Eternity lies in bottomless reservoirs . . . . its buckets
    are rising forever and ever,
They pour and they pour and they exhale away.

We have thus far exhausted trillions of winters and
    summers;
There are trillions ahead, and trillions ahead of them.

Births have brought us richness and variety,
And other births will bring us richness and variety.

I do not call one greater and one smaller,
That which fills its period and place is equal to any.

Were mankind murderous or jealous upon you my
    brother or my sister?
I am sorry for you . . . . they are not murderous or
    jealous upon me;
All has been gentle with me . . . . . . I keep no account
    with lamentation;
What have I to do with lamentation?

I am an acme of things accomplished, and I an
    encloser of things to be.

My feet strike an apex of the apices of the stairs,
On every step bunches of ages, and larger bunches
    between the steps,
All below duly traveled—and still I mount and mount.

Rise after rise bow the phantoms behind me,
Afar down I see the huge first Nothing, the vapor
    from the nostrils of death,
I know I was even there . . . . I waited unseen and
    always,
And slept while God carried me through the lethargic
    mist,
And took my time . . . . and took no hurt from the
    fetid carbon.

Long I was hugged close . . . . long and long.

Immense have been the preparations for me,
Faithful and friendly the arms that have helped me.

Cycles ferried my cradle, rowing and rowing like
    cheerful boatmen;
For room to me stars kept aside in their own rings,
They sent influences to look after what was to hold
    me.

Before I was born out of my mother generations
    guided me,

My embryo has never been torpid . . . . nothing could
   overlay it;
For it the nebula cohered to an orb . . . . the long slow
   strata piled to rest it on . . . . vast vegetables gave it
   sustenance,
Monstrous sauroids transported it in their mouths
   and deposited it with care.

All forces have been steadily employed to complete
   and delight me,
Now I stand on this spot with my soul.

Span of youth! Ever-pushed elasticity! Manhood
   balanced and florid and full!

My lovers suffocate me!
Crowding my lips, and thick in the pores of my skin,
Jostling me through streets and public halls . . . .
   coming naked to me at night,
Crying by day Ahoy from the rocks of the river . . . .
   swinging and chirping over my head,
Calling my name from flowerbeds or vines or tangled
   underbrush,
Or while I swim in the bath . . . . or drink from the
   pump at the corner . . . . or the curtain is down at
   the opera . . . . or I glimpse at a woman's face in
   the railroad car;

Lighting on every moment of my life,
Bussing my body with soft and balsamic busses,
Noiselessly passing handfuls out of their hearts and
    giving them to be mine.

Old age superbly rising! Ineffable grace of dying days!

Every condition promulges not only itself . . . . it
    promulges what grows after and out of itself,
And the dark hush promulges as much as any.

I open my scuttle at night and see the far-sprinkled
    systems,
And all I see, multiplied as high as I can cipher, edge
    but the rim of the farther systems.

Wider and wider they spread, expanding and always
    expanding,
Outward and outward and forever outward.

My sun has his sun, and round him obediently wheels,
He joins with his partners a group of superior circuit,
And greater sets follow, making specks of the greatest
    inside them.

There is no stoppage, and never can be stoppage;
If I and you and the worlds and all beneath or upon
    their surfaces, and all the palpable life, were this

moment reduced back to a pallid float, it would
  not avail in the long run,
We should surely bring up again where we now stand,
And as surely go as much farther, and then farther and
  farther.

A few quadrillions of eras, a few octillions of cubic
  leagues, do not hazard the span, or make it
  impatient,
They are but parts . . . . any thing is but a part.

See ever so far . . . . there is limitless space outside of
  that,
Count ever so much . . . . there is limitless time
  around that.

Our rendezvous is fitly appointed . . . . God will be
  there and wait till we come.

I know I have the best of time and space—and that I
  was never measured, and never will be measured.

I tramp a perpetual journey,
My signs are a rain-proof coat and good shoes and a
  staff cut from the woods;
No friend of mine takes his ease in my chair,
I have no chair, nor church nor philosophy;

I lead no man to a dinner-table or library or
    exchange,
But each man and each woman of you I lead upon a
    knoll,
My left hand hooks you round the waist,
My right hand points to landscapes of continents, and
    a plain public road.

Not I, not any one else can travel that road for you,
You must travel it for yourself.

It is not far . . . . it is within reach,
Perhaps you have been on it since you were born, and
    did not know,
Perhaps it is every where on water and on land.

Shoulder your duds, and I will mine, and let us hasten
    forth;
Wonderful cities and free nations we shall fetch as
    we go.

If you tire, give me both burdens, and rest the chuff
    of your hand on my hip,
And in due time you shall repay the same service
    to me;
For after we start we never lie by again.

This day before dawn I ascended a hill and looked at
the crowded heaven,
And I said to my spirit, When we become the
enfolders of those orbs and the pleasure and
knowledge of every thing in them, shall we be
filled and satisfied then?
And my spirit said No, we level that lift to pass and
continue beyond.

You are also asking me questions, and I hear you;
I answer that I cannot answer . . . . you must find out
for yourself.

Sit awhile wayfarer,
Here are biscuits to eat and here is milk to drink,
But as soon as you sleep and renew yourself in sweet
clothes I will certainly kiss you with my goodbye
kiss and open the gate for your egress hence.

Long enough have you dreamed contemptible
dreams,
Now I wash the gum from your eyes,
You must habit yourself to the dazzle of the light and
of every moment of your life.

Long have you timidly waded, holding a plank by the
shore,

Now I will you to be a bold swimmer,
To jump off in the midst of the sea, and rise again and
    nod to me and shout, and laughingly dash with
    your hair.

I am the teacher of athletes,
He that by me spreads a wider breast than my own
    proves the width of my own,
He most honors my style who learns under it to
    destroy the teacher.

The boy I love, the same becomes a man not through
    derived power but in his own right,
Wicked, rather than virtuous out of conformity or
    fear,
Fond of his sweetheart, relishing well his steak,
Unrequited love or a slight cutting him worse than a
    wound cuts,
First rate to ride, to fight, to hit the bull's eye, to sail a
    skiff, to sing a song or play on the banjo,
Preferring scars and faces pitted with smallpox over
    all latherers and those that keep out of the sun.

I teach straying from me, yet who can stray from me?
I follow you whoever you are from the present hour;
My words itch at your ears till you understand them.

I do not say these things for a dollar, or to fill up the
   time while I wait for a boat;
It is you talking just as much as myself . . . . I act as
   the tongue of you,
It was tied in your mouth . . . . in mine it begins to be
   loosened.

I swear I will never mention love or death inside a
   house,
And I swear I never will translate myself at all, only
   to him or her who privately stays with me in the
   open air.

If you would understand me go to the heights or
   water-shore,
The nearest gnat is an explanation and a drop or the
   motion of waves a key,
The maul the oar and the handsaw second my words.

No shuttered room or school can commune with me,
But roughs and little children better than they.

The young mechanic is closest to me . . . . he knows
   me pretty well,
The woodman that takes his axe and jug with him
   shall take me with him all day,
The farmboy ploughing in the field feels good at the
   sound of my voice,

In vessels that sail my words sail . . . . I go with
    fishermen and seamen, and love them,
My face rubs to the hunter's face when he lies down
    alone in his blanket,
The driver thinking of me does not mind the jolt of
    his wagon,
The young mother and old mother comprehend me,
The girl and the wife rest the needle a moment and
    forget where they are,
They and all would resume what I have told them.

I have said that the soul is not more than the body,
And I have said that the body is not more than the
    soul,
And nothing, not God, is greater to one than one's-
    self is,
And whoever walks a furlong without sympathy
    walks to his own funeral, dressed in his shroud,
And I or you pocketless of a dime may purchase the
    pick of the earth,
And to glance with an eye or show a bean in its pod
    confounds the learning of all times,
And there is no trade or employment but the young
    man following it may become a hero,
And there is no object so soft but it makes a hub for
    the wheeled universe,
And any man or woman shall stand cool and
    supercilious before a million universes.

And I call to mankind, Be not curious about God,
For I who am curious about each am not curious
    about God,
No array of terms can say how much I am at peace
    about God and about death.

I hear and behold God in every object, yet I
    understand God not in the least,
Nor do I understand who there can be more
    wonderful than myself.

Why should I wish to see God better than this day?
I see something of God each hour of the twenty-four,
    and each moment then,
In the faces of men and women I see God, and in my
    own face in the glass;
I find letters from God dropped in the street, and
    every one is signed by God's name,
And I leave them where they are, for I know that
    others will punctually come forever and ever.

And as to you death, and you bitter hug of mortality
    . . . . it is idle to try to alarm me.

To his work without flinching the accoucheur comes,
I see the elderhand pressing receiving supporting,

I recline by the sills of the exquisite flexible doors
    . . . . and mark the outlet, and mark the relief and
    escape.

And as to you corpse I think you are good manure,
    but that does not offend me,
I smell the white roses sweetscented and growing,
I reach to the leafy lips . . . . I reach to the polished
    breasts of melons.

And as to you life, I reckon you are the leavings of
    many deaths,
No doubt I have died myself ten thousand times
    before.

I hear you whispering there O stars of heaven,
O suns . . . . O grass of graves . . . . O perpetual
    transfers and promotions . . . . if you do not say
    anything how can I say anything?

Of the turbid pool that lies in the autumn forest,
Of the moon that descends the steeps of the soughing
    twilight,
Toss, sparkles of day and dusk . . . . toss on the black
    stems that decay in the muck,
Toss to the moaning gibberish of the dry limbs.

I ascend from the moon . . . . I ascend from the night,
And perceive of the ghastly glitter the sunbeams
    reflected,
And debouch to the steady and central from the
    offspring great or small.

There is that in me . . . . I do not know what it is . . . .
    but I know it is in me.

Wrenched and sweaty . . . . calm and cool then my
    body becomes;
I sleep . . . . I sleep long.

I do not know it . . . . it is without name . . . . it is a
    word unsaid,
It is not in any dictionary or utterance or symbol.

Something it swings on more than the earth I
    swing on,
To it the creation is the friend whose embracing
    awakes me.

Perhaps I might tell more . . . . Outlines! I plead for
    my brothers and sisters.

Do you see O my brothers and sisters?
It is not chaos or death . . . . it is form and union and
    plan . . . . it is eternal life . . . . it is happiness.

The past and present wilt . . . . I have filled them and
    emptied them,
And proceed to fill my next fold of the future.

Listener up there! . . . . what have you to confide to
    me?
Look in my face while I snuff the sidle of evening,
Talk honestly, for no one else hears you, and I stay
    only a minute longer.

Do I contradict myself?
Very well then . . . . I contradict myself;
I am large . . . . I contain multitudes.

I concentrate toward them that are nigh . . . . I wait
    on the door-slab.

Who has done his day's work and will soonest be
    through with his supper?
Who wishes to walk with me?

Will you speak before I am gone? Will you prove
    already too late?

The spotted hawk swoops by and accuses me . . . . he
    complains of my gab and my loitering.

I too am not a bit tamed . . . . I too am untranslatable,
I sound my barbaric yawp over the roofs of the world.

The last scud of day holds back for me,
It flings my likeness after the rest and true as any on
     the shadowed wilds,
It coaxes me to the vapor and the dusk.

I depart as air . . . . I shake my white locks at the
     runaway sun,
I effuse my flesh in eddies and drift it in lacy jags.

I bequeath myself to the dirt to grow from the grass
     I love,
If you want me again look for me under your
     bootsoles.

You will hardly know who I am or what I mean,
But I shall be good health to you nevertheless,
And filter and fibre your blood.

Failing to fetch me at first keep encouraged,
Missing me one place search another,
I stop some where waiting for you

EDITOR'S NOTES

GENERAL NOTE

Malcolm Cowley's *Leaves of Grass: The First (1855) Edition*, published in 1959, alerted contemporary readers to the original text of "Song of Myself." His introductory essay contains some insightful pages on the revisions, as does Galway Kinnell's introduction to *The Essential Whitman*. (Mr. Kinnell's book is apparently the first to present a conflated text of "Song of Myself"; I wasn't aware of it until I had completed work on mine.)

I would also like to recommend two excellent essays: "Some Lines from Whitman" in *Poetry and the Age* by Randall Jarrell and "A Draft of Whitman" in *The Gift: Imagination and the Erotic Life of Property* by Lewis Hyde.

TEXTUAL NOTES

The first entry in each note is the revision I have adopted and the date of the edition it comes from (that edition's punctuation, if it differs from the 1855 norm, is indicated within brackets); the second entry is the text of the first edition.

p. xiii, l. 1—Song of Myself: 1876

    1855: no title

p. 4, l. 2—increase, always sex,: 1856

    1855: increase, /

p. 7, ll. 14f.—peace and knowledge: 1867

    1855: peace and joy and knowledge

p. 7, l. 15—all the argument: 1867

    1855: all the art and argument

p. 9, l. 8—old people, or: 1876

    1855: old people and from women, and

p. 12, ll. 6f.—I witness the corpse with its dabbled
hair, I note where the pistol has fallen: 1867
[hair—I].

    1855: It is so . . . . I witnessed the corpse . . . .
there the pistol had fallen.

p. 13, ll. 9f.—I come and I depart.: 1856

    1855: I come again and again.

p. 14, l. 6—Falling: 1867

    1855: Soundly falling

p. 15, ll. 1f.—neck . . . . he held his bride by the hand,:
1867 [neck—he held his bride by the hand;]

    1855: neck, / One hand rested on his rifle . . . .
the other hand held firmly the wrist of the red girl,

p. 15, l. 11—limpsy: 1856

    1855: limpsey

p. 20, l. 22—Thanksgiving: 1860

    1855: thanksgiving

p. 21, l. 22—auction-stand: 1871

   1855: stand

p. 23, ll. 18f.—his first professions,: 1860

   1855: the first professions,

p. 25, l. 17—adobe: 1856

   1855: abode

p. 28, l. 10—behavior: 1860

   1855: behaviour

p. 31, l. 10—Why should I pray? Why should: 1860

   1855: Shall I pray? Shall

p. 31, ll. 12f.—Having pried through the strata and analyzed to a hair, and counselled with doctors and calculated close,: 1860 [Having pried through the strata, analyzed to a hair, counsel'd with doctors and calculated close,]

   1855: I have pried through the strata and analyzed to a hair,

p. 31, l. 14—I find no sweeter fat than sticks to my own bones.: 1860

   1855: And counselled with doctors and calculated close, and found no sweeter fat than sticks to my own bones.

p. 33, l. 13—development: 1856

   1855: developement

p. 37, l. 8—imbuing: 1860

   1855: imbueing

p. 40, ll. 8f.—one thing more than another it shall be the spread of my own body, or any part of it;: 1867 [one thing more than another, it shall be the spread of my own body, or any part of it.]

1855: any particular thing it shall be some of the spread of my body;

p. 45, l. 10—violoncello: 1860

1855: violincello

p. 45, ll. 11ff.—I hear the keyed cornet, it glides quickly in through my ears, it shakes mad-sweet pangs through my belly and breast.: 1856

1855: And hear the keyed cornet or else the echo of sunset.

p. 45, ll. 22f.—It wrenches such ardors from me, I did not know I possessed them,: 1856

1855: It wrenches unnamable ardors from my breast,

p. 46, l. 6—throttled in fakes: 1860

1855: squeezed in the fakes

p. 46, l. 7—At length let: 1860

1855: Let

p. 49, l. 22—chef-d'œuvre: 1860

1855: chef-d'ouvre

p. 50, l. 6—infidels.: 1860

1855: infidels, / And I could come every afternoon of my life to look at the farmer's girl boiling her iron tea kettle and baking shortcake.

p. 50, l. 16—mastodon: 1860
   1855: mastadon
p. 51, l. 5—long and long.: 1867
   1855: sometimes half the day long.
p. 51, l. 15—unhappy: 1876
   1855: industrious
p. 52, l. 6—one that I love,: 1856
   1855: one that shall be my amie,
p. 56, l. 11—apple-peelings: 1856
   1855: apple-pealings
p. 58, l. 8—of Broadway: 1860
   1855: in Broadway
p. 58, ll. 9f—flatting the flesh of my nose on: 1860
   1855: pressing the flesh of my nose to
p. 60, l. 16—We are approaching: 1856
   1855: We are about approaching
p. 61, ll. 21f—well, it: 1856 [well—it]
   1855: well and it
p. 63, l. 16—my fort's: 1856
   1855: some fort's
p. 64, ll. 3f.—damages, making indispensable: 1856
   1855: damages and to make indispensible
p. 67, l. 17—quarter?: 1856
   1855: quarters?
p. 70, l. 16—I embody all presences outlawed or
   suffering,: 1867 [outlaw'd or suffering;]
   1855: I become any presence or truth of humanity
   here,

p. 73, l. 16—naiveté;: 1860 [naïveté]

    1855: naivete;

p. 77, l. 2—Buddha,: 1856

    1855: Adonai,

p. 77, l. 7—Taking: 1856

    1855: Honestly taking

p. 79, l. 8—slues round: 1856

    1855: evolves

p. 80, l. 16—The little plentiful manikins skipping
around: 1867

    1855: They who piddle and patter here

p. 83, ll. 7f.—you, I know the sea of torment, despair
and unbelief.: 1867 [you—I]

    1855: you, and know the unspoken
interrogatories, / By experience I know them.

p. 86, l. 13—fetid: 1860

    1855: foetid

p. 91, l. 21—life.: 1856

    1855: life

p. 94, l. 1—my words sail: 1856

    1855: my words must sail

p. 94, l. 7—old mother comprehend: 1856

    1855: old mother shall comprehend

p. 98, l. 4—there! . . . . what: 1881 [there! what]

    1855: there! Here you . . . . what

SHAMBHALA POCKET LIBRARY

The Dhammapada: A New Translation
of the Buddhist Classic
Translated and edited by Gil Fronsdal

Four Huts: Asian Writings on the Simple Life
Translated by Burton Watson

I Ching: The Book of Change
Translated by Thomas Cleary

The Integral Vision: A Very Short Introduction
Ken Wilber

Kabbalah: The Way of the Jewish Mystic
Perle Besserman

Lovingkindness:
The Revolutionary Art of Happiness
Sharon Salzberg

Meditations
J. Krishnamurti

Mindfulness on the Go
Jan Chozen Bays

The Path of Insight Meditation
Jack Kornfield and Joseph Goldstein

The Pocket Chögyam Trungpa
Compiled and edited by Carolyn Rose Gimian

The Pocket Dalai Lama
Edited by Mary Craig

The Pocket Meister Eckhart
Edited by David O'Neal

The Pocket Pema Chödrön
Edited by Eden Steinberg

The Pocket Rumi
Edited by Kabir Helminski

The Pocket Thich Nhat Hanh
Compiled and edited by Melvin McLeod

The Pocket Thomas Merton
Edited by Robert Inchausti

Siddhartha
Hermann Hesse; translated by Sherab Chödzin Kohn

Song of Myself
Walt Whitman; edited by Stephen Mitchell

The Spiritual Teaching of Ramana Maharshi
Ramana Maharshi

Tao Teh Ching
Lao Tzu; translated by John C. H. Wu

Walden: Selections from the American Classic
Henry David Thoreau

The Wisdom of the Buddha
Compiled and edited by Anne Bancroft

The Wisdom of Tibetan Buddhism
Edited by Reginald A. Ray